Interpretations

50 poems

PAUL H SIMMONS

Interpretations: 50 Poems

Author: Paul H Simmons

Copyright © 2025 Paul H Simmons

The right of Paul H Simmons to be identified as author of this work has been asserted by the author in accordance with section 77 and 78 of the Copyright, Designs and Patents Act 1988.

ISBN 978-1-83538-570-8 (Paperback)

Cover Design and Book Layout by:
    Maple Publishers
    www.maplepublishers.com

Published by:
    Maple Publishers
    Fairbourne Drive, Atterbury,
    Milton Keynes,
    MK10 9RG, UK
    www.maplepublishers.com

A CIP catalogue record for this title is available from the British Library.

All rights reserved. No part of this book may be reproduced or translated by any form or by any means, electronic or mechanical, including photocopying, recording or by any information storage and retrieval system without written permission from the author.

The views expressed in this work are solely those of the author and do not reflect the opinions of Publishers, and the Publisher hereby disclaims any responsibility for them. This book should not be used as a substitute for the advice of a competent authority, admitted or authorized to advise on the subjects covered.

CONTENTS

The interpreter 10

Suggestions 11

Words falling to the ground 12

The sea at full stretch 13

Duality 14

Ebb tide 15

A Land of Abundance 16

Servant of the servants 17

Tahitian Landscape 18

Hosts and Guests 19

Traces 20

A falling face 22

Putting them straight 23

Wiriness 25

An eagle clan 27

Dead weight 28

A suspicion of faith 29

The Second Death 31

Boundaries	32
A built environment	34
Lost voices	36
Knuckling down	38
Life at the sharp end	39
Multitudes	40
A Cathedral City	41
A specialist subject	42
Handiwork	43
Lady Justice	44
Rockers hanging on	45
Elopement (A step too far or a step too late!)	46
A rudimentary step	47
A medley of faith	48
Disparagement	49
A solace	50
The colour of your money	51
Wordsmith forging on	52
A nightmare inside	53

Grace and favour 54

Self-driven, self-made 55

A curtain of rain, a handful of dust 56

No failure allowed 57

Crossed wires 58

Degrees of heat 59

A tree our protector 60

Time and all that 61

Necromancer 62

One last harvest 63

The Young Ladies of Avignon 64

Distance in the soul 65

A Dying Adventure 66

Paul H Simmons

By the same author
A CONSTRUCTION IN SPACE
THE LOOK OF BEAUTY
A VALLEY TO TRAVERSE

For Hannah, Marcus, Isobel, Freddie,
Marie, Vera and Giuliana

All mankind is of one author, and is one volume; when one man dies, one chapter is torn out of the book, but translated into a better language..

Some pieces are translated by age, some by sickness, some by war, some by justice; but God's hand is in every translation, and his hand shall bind up all our scattered leaves again, for that library where every book shall lie open to one another.

John Donne

from Meditation XVII (1623)

The interpreter

He was for all a seer,
as he roamed the London streets,
he wrote and he drew with a timeless art,
words as an image nestled,
and with his hands and with his eyes
he wrought the future, past and present.

A kaleidoscope in deeper shades,
a symmetry that measures,
a balance and a shock of hair
from a potent power brooding;
and all this from the fertile brain
of one whose mind would travel,
showered by the angel train,
in touch with hell and heaven.

Myths and legends multiply,
crouching, floating, healing,
as they shed their rays in the dark of space,
radiant with meaning.

A prophet whose world was a world in flame,
a universe of chaos,
ruled by those forces ever at odds -
but with a heart of pity, and tender looks.

He created them all from a master plan,
from a place unearthly from whence he came,
and with a face at once ghostly
and wildly urbane.

Suggestions

A wretched word reveals us all,
it feasts on someone special;
for to know what we are is to sense where we've been—
and to feel the hurt is a powerful thing.

We knew what was best, but declined to obey,
we were counselled but not in the depths,
we were loved and were sought but forgot to embrace,
turned away to the sullen heavens.

And still we are moved by a loving hand,
into the far beyond,
where suggestions unleash a cradle of hope,
the skies a patchwork of blue,
becoming a shower of deep dark red,
a hint of something new.

Every thought, every sight turns commonplace,
immersed in this light as it fades,
as we swoon in a land of otherness—
where finality is lost in the open space.

Words falling to the ground

So many are lost,
those fashionable words,
the language of today,
and those that were never at once foreseen,
slipping from tongues like rain.

And they fall who knows where,
and they take a turn,
or they ramble as on a path,
nourishing places we've yet to tread,
and reviving the flower we once thought dead.

But the ancient speech was rectified
and prayers not wasted – implored;
for those words they were sent from a mouth to uplift,
then were traced on the desert floor.

The sea at full stretch

It fills the void with a marvellous reach,
    made perfect by its power,
    and when it rages or when it's still,
    we're wrecked or we're buoyed,
    we're shattered or bask so warm;
    such is the balm of its gentleness,
    the cruelty of its storm.

The pearly days on strands and shore,
    the sandiness of wind and salt,
floating about with an eye to the land,
playfully lapped on the arm and the hand,
    and drifting away as far as we dare
    on that substance without compare;
    released by the surge,
    shimmied along by its waves,
swelled by the breeze as a token of strength—
    and added to only by rain.

But there is a creature without a friend,
    lost in a channel of sea,
    where it has been or where it will end
    belongs to the mind of the deep.

And it knows when it's gone,
    when the current devours,
    when it no longer breathes but tastes;
    the salt in a flood
last remembrance of its own unavailing quest.

And the shell for us keeps reminder
    as it coils on a distant beach,
of the passionless depth of the planet's strength,
    when the sea is lapping, but at full stretch.

Duality

We are a dual expression,
we cannot be held on one plane,
the heavens are full as an open door,
and above we command or declare;
with an arm lifted high we sever the air,
and we follow a simple kill;
the fall of an unknown creature,
a songbird that softly thrills.

And the pulse and the throb—
it is up or down,
then in or out it goes,
never a stall or a static note;
and the simple breath of humility,
for our pride is the antidote.

The mystical fear, the mountain's dread,
the grudge of a youth in bed,
it all resolves to a symmetry;
to a flight in the sky,
to the depth of a grave,
to the pity and then the rage,
as a life now spent rests in the end,
just a body disturbing the plane.

And something disrupted humanity,
took the life from the tomb all aglow—
he can't be believed to have woken the dead,
to violate all that we know!

But in his arms was duality,
a man but a person exempt,
breaking the law in a new way,
freeing us all by his death.

Ebb tide

A watershed ridge divides an expanse
where the rivers flow to their sea,
and the glistening stones and the husks and bones
and the shuttling, crooked crabs,
are sucked away where they once were shed,
as the ocean withdraws from its foam to its bed.

And again and again and always,
the trickle becomes the flood,
the one that was known before;
and now it expands to the unknown lands,
to be drawn to another shore,
and the cycle of life seems limitless,
as it unifies once more.

A Land of Abundance

A cactus blooms red in a stony ground,
the incense rises ahead,
a temple is raised from the bedrock,
around and around it grows then it falls,
life in the throes of death,
cries that recall the suffering and blood-flow
wherever we tread.

The Holy of Holies has been defiled,
what is there left to mourn,
the milk and the honey are turned to sand,
and the remnant are lost in a promised land.

They travel alone, they're banished and low,
beaten and left to die,
they carry a load that bears them down,
no home to call their own,
living the life of a stranger,
plagued by the lot they've been thrown.

The land is still there, the people are shed,
regrouping and battening down,
for the storm it will come,
it's already here,
as the kingdom of judgment appears.

A lily of white now flowers in stones,
unfitting it trembles like fear,
and its place in our heart
is broken apart
in this land of abundant tears.

Servant of the servants

An aged man attired in white,
seated quite alone,
trying to shape the human race,
as it struggles to be atoned.

Trying to live life fruitfully,
slowly approaching the end,
murmuring words for the sake of the world,
attended to by the few,
pulsing with sense like a satellite
on its lonely mission above,
circling the globe with a placid face
and a timeless message of love.

He would be gone in an instant,
lost in a hostile world,
but for the time he can rest and express the word,
he can pray and suffer and muse,
kept sane by the bonds of family,
kept afloat by the hope from above.

Magisterial ways defend him,
dense walls try to keep him from harm,
from enemy fire within and beyond,
poor servant of God and of man.

Tahitian Landscape

Delicate stems rise on high,
spider-like growth descends,
leaves that are spiny-primitive,
sky that is densely blue,
clouds so simply treated like puffs of smoke untrue.

The native follows a calling,
yoked down a path on his own,
walking so lightly burdened in grassland burnished and brown.
Absorbed by the vivid colours,
no distinction as mountains beyond,
leaving a landscape behind him,
belonging both here and away,
his back held as an effigy,
immune to the heat of the plain.

The brilliant tracks could lead to the sea,
a ramshackle farm for a home—
pacific life in its essence,
no marble but brittle red stone.

And with every day of the sun-beat,
black dog now setting the way,
he strolls in a new world order,
to shadow pasted by trees,
away from the painter's palette
as he rests with never a breeze,
making the sun speak loudly,
images bold but sheer,
talking to us all in colour,
bringing the south seas so near.

Hosts and Guests

'I was here first, after being away,
eager to join and eager to stay,
and ready to sit as at home';
so the dog took a seat in his basket
and proceeded to chew on his bone.

'But I am high-born, and blessed with a name,
a noble one at that,
and I am a guest since I am so fine,
no contention, the place is all mine'.

So they sat and they ate, above and below,
until a great knock at the gate,
and in file the homeless and workless,
called in from a neighbouring street.

They sat in low places of honour,
and high-born was forced to concede,
the new-born grateful for how they were blessed;
invited and summoned, and passing the test.

They were the truly gentle,
away from the dirt of the past,
while the dog was polite, companion and friend;
first to arrive, and last to depart—
but truly a host to the end.

Traces

From the trees, from the earth there's a vestige,
in the sky looms a section of crane,
stooping alone in its blackness,
behind bushes now masking a lane;
sharpness of steel and blanket of grey,
but nothing resolved, slowly passing away.

Allotments grow many and varied
but mostly the dead life now shows,
season of berries upon us so soon,
flowers the last ones to grow,
while the passion flower senses a victory,
its fruits with a soft orange glow.

I walk in the freedom remotely,
nature my own bosom friend,
remoteness and closeness companions so fair,
stillness of fields as I go,
leaving my mark as a footprint,
noises soft stirring below.

A black flying bird, a dog far away,
the beating of steel on the track,
as a train rattles by to the distance,
and a worker starts to saw -
at the wooden bounds of his real life,
happy to toil as the day fades,
hacking and scraping in the evening shades.

The sounds are the limits of silence
and then they are passed and are gone,
in the dampness of atmosphere stifling
the brightness once nurtured by sun.

Forsaken trees rise on my left,
faint noises of folk nearby,
but never a face well-met;
half-seen through a leaf-blown hedge.

A clearing appears, a hollow so deep
it holds leaves from many a year,
as a squirrel now sheds its trace,
among the clutter of spent things,
and a dead fire once burning ablaze.

The undisturbed in the bushes settle down
into the night,
clicking and rustling within them,
hidden and out of our sight.
A little spinning windmill,
spins on without wind or sound
and all about there is closure
as nature is shuffling down.

The fields are being transformed now,
cut and turned by the plough,
cleanness and smoothness and darkness of clay,
face of the mystery below.
And all things manifest softly,
waiting for movement to grow.

A falling face

A sad and silent girl,
could almost be a child,
wiping empty tables,
lashes boldly styled;
we wish that we could intervene,
lift sorrow from those eyes.

She's fighting with humility,
wrapped against the cold,
pale of face and feature,
lost without a goal.
And what then can we offer her,
tangled in life's threads,
just a smile or friendly word,
not fun but simple sense.

She's plagued by plain futility,
but there will be reward,
and then resumes the struggle,
what she finds at home,
how much the pay affords.

We hope that life flows kindly,
faced by unknown trials,
growing in a cold land,
we hope she finds the warmth,
so many dreams before her,
a drear and daunting task.

We trust she finds a fresh path
out of bleak harm's way,
and someone to hold on to,
filling doubt with peace,
someone to confide in,
to uplift her falling face.

Putting them straight

It seems a vain reprisal
to contradict a friend,
for all we know they may be right,
we seldom see truth in black and white.

We must admit we could be wrong,
for like statistics and their trend,
the number game can mute us all
without a formal lie,
and lead us on the newsreel
or propaganda trail
to doubt the spread of messages,
and set us up to fail.

Where is then the answer bold,
and future with its mystery
that can't be quickly solved?

And then another shedding forth,
as passion takes a hold,
colouring the feeling of a temperamental crowd.
We can't distinguish excellence from clever, slick pretence,
so there is no rebuttal, no vital evidence.

Perhaps we need the right to slay
the waxy, cunning fiend
that dwells within rich palaces
where virtue is unseen.
Or silence dogs that foam at mouth
with unabated rage,
an object of our terror
because they can't be tamed;
or hunt the beast that lives apart
in slums and alleyways.

Many tales turn fiery
and temptation fuels the flames,
we vainly fight the fire with fire –
futile to the end.
It's a dangerous venture,
this life without a mind,
this life without a voice;
we barely know what we should think,
not to mention sound advice.

But turn again to parables
with meanings imprecise,
messages of love and hope
speaking from within;
then we find a certainty,
a touch from knowing friend,
putting straight the enemy,
scourging every sin.

Wiriness

A cat is as wiry as they come,
it climbs and it spits and it claws,
not like a flaccid human,
or one as fit as can be,
built for the battle or for the games
but ill at ease in a gnarled old tree.

Or even a mobile monkey,
at stretch wherever he goes,
you wouldn't call him wiry,
he's more the flexible type;
and a dog is a different customer,
in the wild more up for a fight,
at home more inclined to eat.

A fish you can't call it wiry,
it may be sharp of tooth,
but its silky, slippery body
is really far too smooth.

But there is a man with sinews,
hot-wired in the head,
one whose thoughts and actions
are like the fabled cat;
his eyes are black and small and deep,
complexion red and grey,
but he is a beast of the human race,
proving we're not dead,
latching on to theories,
filled with sharp ideas,
quick to fight his corner,
but merciful and kind;

hope enduring still,
brave when it comes to the end,
holding on and staring,
a trifle mad but a cat's best friend.

An eagle clan

An even-tempered power
above a fragile store
of widely-gaping, grasping things,
a strength that sees then soars;
a brood that moves expectantly,
urging for a place,
below a mother's tenderness,
the mighty wings' embrace.

She hovers close, but abstract,
a care we can't express,
warm air fanning particles
of sun-kissed golden dust
and filaments and feathers,
touching without touch.

Like an angel with bent face,
stooping in a wilderness -
movement as a constant
with piercing distant eye -
she is love without a name,
a maker in the sky.

Dead weight

We try to move so lightly
or muse about a cloud,
or comprehend a rainbow
or fathom what was heard;
but everywhere we're bound down,
the senses fail to work,
because we're full of body,
that tragic, painful load;
and in all walks we're limping
and in all thoughts we're marred
by the failure of this instrument
we just can't do without.

Many times it benefits,
the pain or discontent,
this suffering and weakness
can help us represent
the best that we can offer,
some kind of second sense -
but why should we need trouble
within our mortal frame
to make us make an utterance
that stands the test of time
or rise above our nature,
fighting nature all the time?

A suspicion of faith

It can sense unreasoned faith,
our vessel formed with clay,
but without love it wearies,
without hope it fades.
And we can own a swathe of land,
a handsome territory,
but without care it's eaten up,
the poison darnel grows,
and empty tracks lead our poor steps,
where brackish water flows.

The soul is on an errand,
it finds when all seems lost,
a purpose pulls it onward,
dead pools become so clear,
rivers now have meaning,
fallow fields restore.

From appetite it gathers,
from haunts so far below,
from barren land now water
helps the hunger grow.

But then a stark reminder
tempts us to retreat,
doubts and superstitions
lead us on through fear
to otherworldly places,
and dryness reappears.

At once a sense of action,
that purpose once again,
to seize what we are offered
before it is quite gone.

But even if we falter and fail
and quite despair,
there is true restoration -
and love is always there.

The Second Death

At the first we're quietly born
into life anew
and water is the essence
and oil a symbol too.
We have a fellow feeling,
as clothed afresh we grow,
with little robin mothers,
or eaglets jostling through,
innocent in essence
to taste the worm below.

And then the life encounter,
the choice or lapse we make -
there must be ways to navigate
the deadly burning lake.
And at the last there's reckoning,
a Gilead to climb,
the good the bad and heinous
will then all be revealed;
but what have we to answer,
where have we to go,
and do we have to suffer
for what was never known?

Boundaries

I don't see a country,
I see a vital place,
not a hive of people,
or megalopolis,
but somewhere where the bees can swarm,
the plains hear distant beat
of wild and eager horses,
their noise in far retreat.
Or miles and miles of forest
stretching out of sight
and meeting with horizons;
there's a true release,
a barrier no longer,
no check-point to police.

I don't see a country,
divided by the wars
or sown with different people
with untold ways or laws;
but I see a landscape,
formed long before our time,
a rugged place with pastures,
expanse of lonely dales,
animals long grazing,
grass and flowers wild.
This is true expansion,
but our eyes are blind,
for we don't cherish beauty;
we damage distant skies.

I don't see a country,
even with its tracks,
for these become a roadway
or railroad for the train
and on high we see the runway,
tarmac for the plane.
These routes are going somewhere
within a hidden plan,
departures and arrivals,
a place of safe return.
But I would travel lonely
without a place to go,
to see the river passing -
wild border in its flow.

A built environment

There can be keen adventure
though in towers by rows of trees,
in stone and steel and artifice,
in glass that pierces high,
a match for any landscape,
too much for the naked eye.
The light it seems to swivel
as we gaze on a broken space;
and this we build,
make bridges to join a foreign land,
the noise and haste about us,
the sun at hazy play
while inside we are cushioned
and light can mimic day.

Without some kind of shelter
we fail and nothing lasts,
but only when we mould it,
suited to the heart -
a cover for our frailty
the natural world imparts.
Building gently shields us,
protects us as we fall,
gives us warmth and impulse,
safe home when darkness grows,
a place for fragile artwork
or wardrobe for our clothes.
Even shanty town and shacks,
they form a kind of bond,
the rain disturbs and harries them,
but solace can be found.

Cityscape or landscape,
the two can be as one;
as we peer into the distance,
the prospect may be wild or twisted
into buildings, leaping to the sky
or laid out as a tapestry,
colourless and grey,
silhouette at nightfall,
glistening in the day.
A dome where lie some grandees
in alabaster tombs,
the comforting and playful performance
in the round, gestures of the pantomime,
imitating all, or a solitary dancer
within a massive hall.

Lost voices

They whispered as they loved me,
they cared and smiled beside,
and later they upheld me
with justice on my side.
The speech in measured tones of law,
the gentle talk at ease,
but they were never memories,
voices such as these.

And how will they be registered
now that they are past,
a record only plays a tune
if we retrieve the song,
otherwise discarded and left to wait alone.
And will they still retain a place,
when mine is lost and gone?

Those sounds of early childhood,
those words of later years,
the lifted prayer, the anger,
all lodged without a trace.
But deep within our membrane of life
we own the joy of hearing
what's familiar, long gone but still nearby.
It's as if we know them, but unsure of where they've been,
these many years of silence make old expressions dim.

But sometimes like a movie,
a summer holiday,
the words at first seem muted,
the places bright and gay;
then the noise and soundtrack,

faces, speech we know,
from the sunny uplands, so clear yet long ago.

Or all the mass of images
within a social crowd,
those who once were schoolboys,
their voices like today;
but when the future changes,
when they are old and grey,
is what we knew still valid,
will we hear or recognise,
will we lose those dear reminders,
or find them by and by?

Knuckling down

Such is the essential, this work we must endure;
we never gain a foothold, buy the baby's gown,
without some form of effort, we must be knuckling down.
But what a complication, to face the harsh terrain,
when we're still chasing shadows all over our domain;
it may be small and humble, we want to sit and dream,
but without occupation, without the daily round,
life pursues its misery, abasement is the theme.

But knuckling down it pains us; it may be also said
that many toils and troubles prepare and feed the ground;
the seeds of small beginnings, the many vacant hours,
what we don't accomplish, what we start and fail,
journeys now forsaken, paths we dare not tread –
defer for us temptation on life's uncoiling thread;
and pull us ever closer to where we're bound to be;
for we're always going somewhere, even the somewhere
we can't see.

Life at the sharp end

We sometimes sleep so soundly, enfolded by the night,
while sirens in the slip road or beacons flashing bright
unleash the life of anger, the damage and the loss,
the symbol of an accident, the tearing of our flesh,
the wreckage of the aftermath, the stormy, nightly mess.

And those who care intensely and seek to mollify
what can't be gently treated, what can't be rectified;
the bones and blood of ages, the violence that we spread -
this is the sharpest pain that nature can express.

Multitudes

They push and flock in silence upon the city streets,
no hint of inner gladness, no children to be seen;
black garmented and ghastly they crowd the nightly scene,
the lights are merely troublesome, the rain so sharp it stings,
and doorways to the eateries are lined then crammed within.

A higher, vacant entrance must lead to somewhere grand,
escape from drenching water, great koi so close-confined,
a sense of tainted luxury, a welcome half-refined.
A crafty little look as if to deprecate and then
expansive tables, a space to sit and wait –
for guests and old acquaintance, the warmth a welcome break.

A table slow-revolving, dumb-waiter to attend,
or maybe lazy Susan, the maid without appeal,
who takes a servant's order, numbered with no plan,
no aid or explanation to help us understand.

But we are somewhere set apart, and culture flows so wide,
only interrupted by the sudden tourist tide;
a stranger down in Soho she lays a place for us,
so let us be receptive, not harbour cold mistrust,
and we shall find humanity where it could be lost.

For this is multi-London, a place for one and all,
a place for all to taste, and in a dark and rainy evening
we join the multitude, but push for something better -
a home for solitude.

A Cathedral City

There's a warm and tranquil welcome within a sacred space,
one where lost nobility, once regal, now at rest,
lives on without a whisper, a taper prayer at best –
whose smoke now soft diffuses and flames glow on till night,
while vapours of dark ages incense the airy heights.

Such a new sensation, to feel the ancient stone,
to touch the hands before us by touching what has grown
into deep maturity, into golden light,
from a state of emptiness into something bright.
The sun itself is happy to cast a coloured eye
upon the citizens in rows or those whose anthems flow
toward the seat of heaven, its hidden, mighty throne.

And we are touched by silence or sometimes with a song
within this gentle monument, within this holy home –
where wood may burn, but never ends the birth of something new,
adorned and dressed in beauty its fabric through and through.

And this is where a city, teeming and intense,
finds its heart of stillness, its face of innocence.
We long for those environs, we're drawn from near and far –
to a symbol and a statement, true sense of who we are.

A specialist subject

There are a host of experts who understand a lot
of what the world can offer, of what there is to learn,
so much, a thousand pages, a weighty magazine,
or e-zine to all continents; while they retain a slice,
a sliver of the magnitude of data-crowded life.

And do we know where knowledge rests, where they may find their clues
that seem to validate their thought, to seem omniscient?
They have in fact assurance, and we are reassured
by the handling of a subject which teaches all mankind
about that little something that we could never find.

And as the soulful thinker dreams, and tries to contemplate,
the flight of random atoms lost, at last can find a place.
For to be a sage takes wisdom, to understand the plan,
to take a piece of knowledge and know where it may fit,
within the wider puzzle formed by some strange hand.

Handiwork

It takes a thousand hands, it seems, to fashion ancient wares
or cut into a mountain, grow produce from the land,
as perched upon an outcrop we gaze on years of toil,
castles of immensity, houses clustered on a hill.

The handiwork of nature still more it has to tell,
for we are only dwellers within a wider space,
one that stretches seamless from earth to sea and sky,
and we have just a portion of all that we can see,
but also skill and power, collective energy.

How does a mighty bridge take shape, how does it span the air,
we never saw a movement, but suddenly it's there?
How do the ant-like creatures coalesce and flow and form
with calloused hands the steel, the substance that we know.
Or hand down through the ages those megaliths of stone?

Lady Justice

There is no shred of evidence that hides from blinded sight,
and every revelation that true enquiry makes
is weighed by hands impartial, a justice lady-like.
Without misshapen weakness or a fatal flaw,
without the fear or favour that everywhere conspires
to break the spell of nature that nature casts entire –
the tide of life is minded to settle every score,
but in a manner peaceful, restraining at a glance,
subduing what is reckless, restoring what's undone,
unveiling what was chance.

Like a steady hourglass that holds within a grain
the treasure of time passing, then turns and starts again,
the law in train is captured by walls, a virtual shield -
but the process of the courtroom is null without appeal.
For all the scribes and jurists, the reams of futile deeds,
can't extract a verdict or contradict a claim
made in the heat of conflict where words and passions flame.
The lasting final judgment, though, surpasses every thought,
every well-versed plan; for nature through the psyche flows,
at odds with fallen man.

Rockers hanging on

The beat is from a haggard bunch of rockers in their time,
in a café rolling on, eclipsed by one who shines,
fronting with the rhythm, steady soulfulness,
an afro style in leather with vibrancy adorned,
he sways and sings so joyfully - to the manner born.

And in the shade old rockers, hacking at their strings,
faces gaunt and wizened, somehow hanging on,
a life of living only for living on the run;
they're nodding and declining, they're mild but lightly stoned,
with their leader now demoted to a table on his own.
From there he strains for limelight, encouraging his crew,
mouthing something mouthy, flailing arm above,
round and round his hand incites the energy they've lost.

Elopement (A step too far or a step too late!)

Many times envisaged this flight from daily grind,
to take a hand and run so fast away from all we've seen,
upon a wingèd chariot or carriage in the snow,
in dark of night to feel the ice, escape from all we've known.

Perhaps a local drifting, though, a muted fanfare blast,
a temperate endeavour within our own estate,
without the night of danger and all it implicates.
For who would tend the everyday once it was left behind,
who would greet us when we taste those new exotic climes?
And would our rose bush still be there that flowers out of time?

A rudimentary step

Clinging on to someone we make our first misstep
And in the dim beginning was the first attempt
The floor is somewhere hazardous
The rails they move like fate
But who had Eve to guide her?
Who Adam to embrace?
For to trust the hand that leads us
Could be our first mistake.

A medley of faith

Be the Anabaptist, revoke the modern world,
start us off in adulthood, skip the little child;
become a modern Baptist, and wash the body clean,
or wash the feet from ages gone; advance a Quaker's dream.

Or turn quite Pentecostal, speak to us in tongues,
make a prohibition to keep us all from harm,
be so strict, particular, and close us in as one.
Or look to Charismatics, a gift they have to praise;
evangelise the world entire within the mission field
and lead your men to martyrdom, a triumph from the grave.

Why not employ a method, revive, renew with form,
and lead the fervent people from sin and deep decline,
or meet in congregation, to plough a furrow as we may,
not led by priests, but prophets, to find the Bible way?

And then the more established field, so Anglican at heart,
so liberal it hurts you, so stern the other part.
They have all the assets now but Catholics on the move
are creeping in so boldly, they've really found a home,
and have authentic teaching, retold and shaped by Rome.

So mix them up and shake them, mind you stir them well,
these faiths, denominations, there's little way to tell
which has the finer programme, which is the safer guide
to offer true admonishment, escape from hell beside.

Disparagement

It's funny to consider all things we ridicule,
all types we undermine, in pursuit of laughter,
in trivial exchange with all things entertaining;
but now we draw a line - we don't offend our neighbour
if he is compromised, we don't provoke an audience
with mean or hurtful lies - sometimes too we're mindful
of a presence from above, and what is true we seldom mock
the purest form of love.

Funny isn't it…

A solace

The soundlessness about us is felt when music fails
but both are bound together, a language that's in use,
a sentence sometimes lingering upon the human breath,
a song that seems to settle when all the world's at rest.

A comfort and a measure of what it feels to taste
the melodies long-playing, swelling with deep tone,
rising to the altitudes, easing every pain.
A tuba or a violin, somehow intertwined,
the light and brassy music, at rest again in time.

The colour of your money

It seems to have no substance, this money that we make,
with no intrinsic value, no cost, no estimate;
because the balance-keeping, that long-drawn balance sheet,
disappears in formless drifts, as the leaves now shed,
that gently float and gather, then sink to murky depths.

The calculated numbers, the words upon a cloud,
they fall and seep within the margins of one connected mind.
Those symbols, lines and phrases in monetary ways,
those fractions of a salary, or messages once clad
in outdated terms and columns, in colours that have bled -
an eye for numbers gleaning now only emptiness.

For they're like figures tumbling and dragged so deep below,
the ink on sheets of water, it percolates within;
while bankruptcy and affluence they rest there all beside
those sodden notes of paper, now quite unclassified.

'Here lies One
Whose Name was writ in Water'
Feb 24th 1821

Gravestone of John Keats in Rome

Wordsmith forging on

He balances the magic to make those humble things,
a blacksmith bending over a cast of metal ware,
the iron wrought and stretching, growing with the fire,
he kneels and prays for ever but never strides above,
fashioning his object from the embers of his love.

And so too from the smithy of words we're dreaming of,
the burning of sensation reverts to fragile type,
but strengthened by the message, the mixture and the style,
and beaten into rising, if only for a while,
for then it forms and settles, the picture of a mind.

If words of love and hope and hate could cast their image
on a page, without the need for grammar or concepts crowding by,
it would be easy writing, without the search for lines,
as we watch a locksmith prising open doors,
revealing all so slowly a lighter verse inside.

A nightmare inside

An insect life is better than man's own bitter sting,
he pulls around for ever, he's trapped within a noose,
the life is straining, draining, sinking from within,
the pain he knows is deadly, and for a while he breathes,
but can't contain the pressure, the fiend that cries for peace.

He lies so deep, profoundly, in what would once be sleep,
but he is moved by visions, the evilness of dreams,
with horizons of the outcast, a grey, unchanging screen
that moves without perception, without being seen.

He tries to rise on impulse, but movement is a threat,
he's trapped within a threshold, one step would be in hell,
retreat can't save him now. And so like pinioned insect
he's tied into a cage, with windows to the outside
but nowhere else to see, lying there so tightly,
but always to be seen.

Grace and favour

Privilege, entitlement, but given in good faith,
not destined for unworthiness, but handed on a plate –
gentle arms around you, a loving, giving plate.
You may find quiet contentment, living others' lives,
lodged with peace around you, sheltered from the crowd.

It may be well deserved, this mansion with no fee,
a place of honest welcome, of deep security.
But all the while the forest grows around the noble pile,
the darkness gathers gloomily, the calls of night resound,
and grand accommodation harbours doubts of troubled kind.

Society is fickle, position never sure,
what is offered freely can be taken back once more;
honesty it staggers, forces stir unrest,
but losing all is nothing, if it can be replaced.
Take a lonely cottage to match the greater place,
keep the steady income, retire and taste the best,
for grace and favour honours sit well with humbleness.

Self-driven, self-made

Nothing can contain us, we're on the open road,
driven by those forces, protected by far more,
our introverted passion is sure of who we are;
when we're ploughing onward, when we're speeding far,
remotest doubt it never shakes the sleek and shining car;
the road it stretches onward, but others interfere,
those who now are journeying within a slower lane,
or shifting on the jay-walk to find another side,
lost within the mayhem, progress in its tide,
going places always but turned by what impels;
the urge they have inside.

And power rises brightly, but sets when all is done,
and earthly-bound it finds itself in boardrooms at the desk,
in mind-set of the maker, in charts that map success,
developed from the schoolroom which sorts the poor from best.
Challenges seem worthy, dedication too,
to persevere is virtue, to search for what is true.
But do we drift with lost direction as we navigate our move,
trusting independence, that unlikely truth?
For we rely on others, formed by others too,
and where we go and what we are emits from spheres so far,
planted in the conscience, and watered by the stars.

A curtain of rain, a handful of dust

We penetrate a sanctuary, dim but now revealed,
with sound of water running and channels to the side,
a rivulet long-rippling its way to future life.
We answer then so slowly some softer water's call
and enter now more deeply, entranced by sacredness,
the vessels and the altar, a taste for living bread.

Until we see before us, like entrance to a cave,
a sheet of falling water, a curtain there of rain.
We wash ourselves entirely, and tear the veil we must,
laden with our treasure, gained at such a cost;
particles just like the sand, handfuls of our dust.

No failure allowed

In our low condition we make our own mistakes
but cruelty is rampant, words a deadly blow,
where indiscretion taints us, and love is never blind,
a kiss becomes an outrage, and prayer is a crime;
while calumny and libel they stalk bewildered minds.

If we choose to acquiesce, if we hold our tongue,
when all about are looking out for what we might have done,
and seeking restitution for what was never wrong;
then we submit to failure and tow the party line,
admit that when examined the test just can't be passed -
without a new beginning, without a second chance.

Crossed wires

Loosen up your language, dampen down your style;
retreat from flowing, rhyming line, adapt and taste the new,
making sense of openness where words they hang around,
curious, more curious this modern world we've found.

Let go of comprehension, leave space for randomness,
don't pack your words too densely, avoid the mild refrain,
don't simplify your meaning, nor wrap those lines again.
But is this all illusion, this liberty we claim,
do the words that bind us, the words we tend to write,
impede us then and hinder the passage taking flight?

And when the message lies entwined upon a folded page,
does it make for wires that cross or do those wires make strong
the meaning and the essence of what is moved along?
Go and sever sharply those threads that bind so tight
and they explode with energy, they leave you unconfined,
but confronted with a blankness, this novelty we find.

Rhyme, rhythm and repetition; maybe this is poetry after all,
for better or for worse…

Degrees of heat

Shuttered in an ice-hut, adrift on eastern plains,
the tundra frozen solid, a mammoth in its pit,
prison camp in wilderness where cabins burst with steam,
the heavens which can never heat, even from the stars,
as space stands vast and empty, infinity at large.

A mountain where the air is thin, the leopard in its cave,
wrested from the rocks its prey, limp and dry within.
The antelope in winter's chase, white fox in frigid den,
the words that form on others' lips, they chafe and burn again.

Those once made for frost and snow, for trawling bitter seas,
they now transform in sunshine, revive in summer heat.
With coloured dreams of paradise, we find and bless the warmth,
enraptured by a better place, with softer tongue we talk.

Paul H Simmons

A tree our protector

It is a sure protector, not a lightweight guard,
the tree that stands like monument, a testament to age;
for ages past we've reminisced below its willing boughs,
or sheltered where the sun refrains or rain drips on for hours.
It breaks in two from out the earth, great struts that rise and form,
the tender leaf, the filigree, the canopy that's born.

If we could glimpse its early days and greenery when young,
the place where it seemed absent, surroundings now long gone;
if we could see beginnings, as well as rounded girth,
the way that others dawdled by, no thought for mother earth,
the way that all those grasses grew before the ancient stock;
then lesser things would matter more within the timeless plot.

Time and all that

If you can wait for time to pass, that may be patience
If you can work and persevere, you may see the light
If you plan to catch a dream, the dream will surely fly
If you have something to show for something said

—You may well be dead.

Necromancer

Couch and curtains, velvet night and mystic candle burns;
this the room where all dreams count and there can be revealed,
whether they a prison make or joyless spread of grey,
or psychedelic fantasy that's nebulized, expelled,
in colours that grow shimmering, in fears that are withheld.

He tries to shake us, then break loose those arcane memories,
tries to bind the heat of us, release it with our grief,
to wrench the very softness and heal what he defines -
as hypnotist or doctor, therapist or friend,
examiner of mind – to feel our conscious bias
or deep subconscious well of powerful imaginings,
our trust, our guilt, our will.

He beholds us vandalised, damaged from the past,
or the present happenings, diseases of our thought,
in time of balanced jeopardy, in place of last resort.
Is it virtual magic though, and do we risk our soul,
in handing over custody of our most precious thing,
the mystery of the inner self, the realm we want to shun,
to one who sits so comfortably, who smiles at brokenness,
who delves within our senseless selves - to raise the living dead?

One last harvest

We cut the tree of ages, we fell the tree of hope,
the haul of Christmas berries, the red upon the white,
and all things growing tapered and reaching far beyond
the overlaying greenness, the frost of valley floor,
now relinquish quickening to dwell in homes once more.

And like to them our seed time, once spread and fanned abroad,
at last it gathers goodness, with hope it burgeons forth,
becoming at the end-time a harvest from the field,
not cut so prematurely though, an everlasting yield.

The Young Ladies of Avignon

This was never borrowed, an image to give back,
or copied from another source, a lesser type of rage,
if anything he steals it from the primal world,
disguises and contortions, the primitive beside the lonely
and appealing, empty worker girls, with eyes that look acutely,
one rolling to the side.

And draped is the attendant there, Egyptian-like she stands,
without the taste of glamour though, and disembodied hand;
above its touch is empty, reality laid bare,
within this house of decadence, where dark attacks blue light,
the fruit that never tempts us, the mask that stares dog-like.

Distance in the soul

If we could see inside a head, the closer we may be,
but always there is distance between the you and me,
between the us and them, between the he and she.
And what we may discover when we have crawled inside
may not be so uplifting, a wealth of tears and shame,
items of a lesser place, things we wouldn't own,
things we wouldn't testify till every law is known;
those that stand there naked, which before were clothed;
uncovering is primitive, we can't expect to show
a memory that haunts us, the secrets young and old.

A Dying Adventure

Everywhere about us the groans of dying toll,
from sharpest and acutest, to bedside slow release,
we never know the answer to what we're living through,
we may not ever find it, leave the world and never taste
the passage of our latter days, the low or ringing cry,
the food of our last supper, our very own demise.

This could be adventure then, to search for what becomes
of some sweet work endeavour, and afternoons of sun,
or bitter times and lonely ones, winter never gone.
It could be education then, to wish our last farewell,
to glimpse our last goodbye, before the ship of life sails on
to greater seas and sky, bringing revelation then,
a flash of life entire.

www.ingramcontent.com/pod-product-compliance
Lightning Source LLC
Chambersburg PA
CBHW041228070526
44584CB00006B/329